Dear Parent,

In <u>Why Is It Cold?</u> your child will learn how air temperature and strong winds make cold weather. Mr. Fox uses a weather map, a thermometer, a weather vane, and other instruments to explain cold weather. Don't forget to brrr-ing your jacket as you turn the page.

Sincerely,

Rita D. Gould

Managing Editor

FAMILY FUN

- Make a winter mobile. Help your child draw and cut out winter-weather symbols—snowflakes, clouds, icicles, mittens, scarf, hat—from construction paper. Attach a piece of string to the top of each symbol and tie the strings to a coat hanger. Hang the mobile from the ceiling.

- Make a cool picture collection. Help your child cut from old catalogs and magazines pictures that show winter scenes and sports—people dressed warmly, snow activities, skiing, sledding, ice skating. Help your child make a collage by pasting the pictures on a piece of paper.

READ MORE ABOUT IT

- *What Are Seasons?*
- *Why Is It Hot?*
- *Why Do Animals Sleep Through Winter?*

WEEKLY READER BOOKS presents

Why Is It Cold?

A **Just Ask**™ Book

Hi, my name is Christopher!

by Chris Arvetis
and Carole Palmer

illustrated by
Vernon McKissack

FIELD PUBLICATIONS
MIDDLETOWN, CT.

I can show you more about cold weather with my weather map.
We can find out where our cold weather begins.
Look at the X.

The cold north wind moves
across the land.
It pushes the warm air
out of the way.

Sometimes the cold air
causes clouds to form
in the sky.

Water in the clouds gets
colder and colder.

It often turns to ice.

When the ice gets heavy,
it falls to the earth
as snow.

Let's look at the weather map again.
The cold air from the north moves across the land.

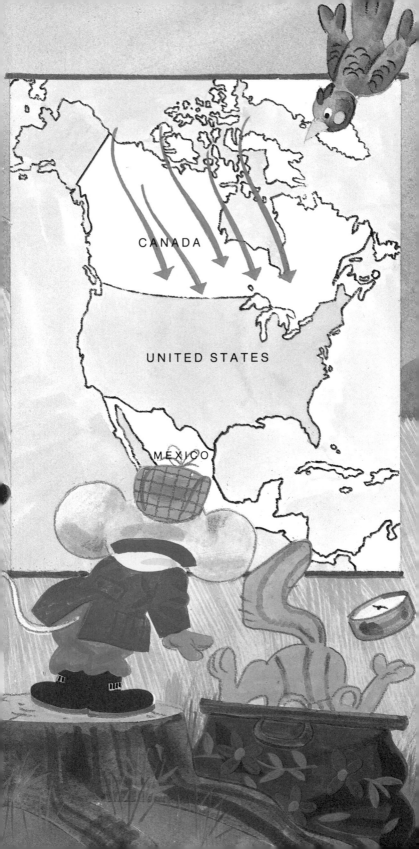

The temperature drops lower and lower.